DEDICATION

I dedicate this book to my family and friends!
Thanks for your support!

The Ten Commandments to a Financial Healing

Kemberley Washington, CPA

www.21daysof.com

Copyright © 2015 Kemberley Washington, CPA
All rights reserved.
ISBN-13: 978-1499607260

Table of Contents

Preface 7

How to use this book 9

Introduction 10

How to obtain a financial healing 12

Commandment # 1 – Put God first in your finances 16

Commandment # 2 – Plan for your financial future 22

Commandment # 3 – Let your budget inspire you 28

Commandment # 4 – Be prepared for what tomorrow brings 34

Commandment # 5 – Be the lender and not the borrower 40

Commandment # 6 – Don't hide your money in a napkin 46

Commandment # 7 – Let your finances be decent and in order 53

Commandment # 8 – Be faithful over little 59

Commandment # 9 – Don't cheat on your taxes 65

Commandment # 10 – Make wiser financial decisions 71

Conclusion 79

About the author 85

Preface

After writing my first book, *21 Days of Powerful Breakthroughs*, I knew it was now time to complete a book regarding finances. I had always purposed in my heart to write a book about finances and as a matter fact, I began this book prior to starting and completing my first book! But it finally all made sense. Had I not completed *21 Days of Powerful Breakthroughs*, I would not have had the confidence and motivation to complete and write other books.

So as I began to gather my thoughts, I began to seek God's face by declaring a fast. The thought came to me after reading the book of Esther. It outlined several key points. As you are familiar with the story of Esther, before she started the mission of saving her people, she first prayed and fasted, planned and more importantly she used her God given talents and gifts to bring her mission to pass.

During this time of fasting, God began to also convict me in areas that I thought I was doing okay in. He led me to close all credit card accounts and my bank account's overdraft protection. He desired for me to build a cash reserve to utilize in the event of unexpected expenses. This was challenging for me because I had three or four credit cards that I relied upon for emergencies. Although, at this point, I kept little to no balances, I kept them around because it provided me a sense of financial security. However God reminded me, He was my source and protection (Psalm 18:2 NKJV). So I chose to trust in Him regarding my finances. And now as I look back, I understand this lesson wasn't just for my financial benefit, but it has and continues to be a blessing to so many others who are struggling with debt and finances.

But please understand, God personally instructed me to "let go" of my credit cards. He may instruct you to do the same or something else. This is why it is so important for you to be sensitive to God's voice, because only He knows your situation. I can testify. I never trusted God so much as my provider as I do now. It is through Him I am blessed and am able to be a blessing to others.

I pray and hope the passages throughout this book are a blessing to you just as much as they have been a blessing to me. **I have and continue to stand on the concept of first allowing God to write through me and then using what I write to help others! So just as you learn from my writings, I too have learned from them as well. Be blessed and financially healed!**

How to use this book

If you ever attended one of my classes, you understand quickly that I believe in the power of numbers. So much so, that I encourage each person who attends to pray and select an accountability partner. The Bible also reminds us that there is power in numbers. In Matthew 18:20 it tells us when two or more are gathered together in His name, Jesus Christ of Nazareth is in the midst.

As you devote ten days to reading, please commit to praying and fasting as well. If you are seeking a healing as it relates to your finances, be reminded that Matthew 17:21 tells us some things only come by prayer and fasting.

Lastly, select a time that works for you and your accountability partner to discuss the reflection questions and devotions periodically. Consider using my book, *Are you wearing the B.A.D.G.E.®? Financial Planner* to keep your finances in order. Ponder on ways to determine what steps can be made to become better financial stewards and obedient to Him in the area of your finances.

My accountability partner

Name: _____

Contact Info: _____

Introduction

If Jesus came back today and said to you, "Give me $500 and I will open the gates of heaven to you," would you be able to receive His blessings? Or, would you have to go to Fast Cash Payday for a payday loan?

Many of us have far too often spent more than what we save. From youth, most of us are instructed to do things such as make good grades or avoid the use of drugs, but less often are we taught to budget or use credit cards wisely. The majority of the time, our spending habits are on depreciable items, such as cars, clothing, and jewelry. By no means, am I saying give up on spending on such items. Hey! You must enjoy life sometimes! But what I am saying is if we can make corporations wealthy, why not make our future generations and ourselves wealthy as well.

A good man leaves an inheritance to his children's children, but the wealth of the sinner is stored up for the righteous.

(Proverbs 13:22)

From this day forth, commit yourself to becoming a better financial steward and you will receive God's financial healing for your life. This will only be accomplished by committing to make small steps and sacrifices to change your financial picture. Just as if you were seeking to complete a college degree, or lose a couple of pounds, you have to remain diligent and steadfast. I promise after awhile you will start to see a change.

I know you are saying, "I don't make any money. My family can barely make ends meet right now." And you may be right. I don't know your situation, but I am a living testimony that financial situations can change. I once was also a victim of spending. I lacked savings and used to hide from my creditors. I can recall a time in my college days attempting to purchase a car and my credit score was below 400! The car salesman stated there would be no chance I would ever get a loan.

After graduating from college, I made a strong commitment to get my finances in order. I have to first let you know my secret weapon – tithing. There is really no other way around it. In the beginning, I gave up a few times when I didn't fully trust God. In those times, however God showed me that disobedience cancels blessings. As a result, I fully committed to the tithing principle and have tithed ever since. The Bible instructs us to bring the tithes to the storehouse. He will pour out a blessing that you do not have room enough to receive (Malachi 3:10). This is true not only in our finances but God will help us in all areas of our lives when we are faithful with our tithes.

How to obtain a financial healing

Oftentimes, I speak about a financial healing, but what is truly a financial healing?

I believe a financial healing is getting into a place where you are no longer:

- Dodging your bill collectors;
- Apprehensive about running your credit report;
- Worried about your financial future or achieving your financial goals;
- Spending beyond your means;
- Misappropriating the finite amount of resources that God has blessed you with; and
- Your savings account is no longer running on empty!

And more importantly, you move into a place where you not only put God first in your life, but you put Him first concerning your finances, seek His wisdom and partner with Him through your giving.

Now before you read in any further, I believe there is something you should know.

Having a financial healing doesn't necessarily mean that you would become an instant millionaire. If this does happen, please don't forget to call me (smile)!

But, what it does mean is that you get into a place where you can have peace, assurance, and trust that everything will be okay concerning your finances.

Can this happen overnight?

Maybe. Maybe not.

Will it require a journey? In most cases – yes. But I think that it is a journey that is well worth it and will not only be a blessing to you but those around you as well.

So, before we explore the true meaning of a financial healing, I need to ask you a few questions:

Reflection Questions

1. What does a financial healing means to you?

_____
_____
_____
_____

2. What do you believe has stopped you from obtaining your financial healing?

_____
_____
_____
_____

3. What area has God convicted you concerning your finances that you have chosen to ignore?

_____
_____
_____
_____

4. During this time of reading and fasting, what can you give up as a sacrifice to obtain a financial healing?

_____
_____
_____
_____

Notes:

Commandment # 1 - Put God first in your finances

Scripture Reading: "Bring all the tithes into the storehouse, that there may be food in my house, and try me now in this," says the Lord of hosts, "If I will not open for you the windows of heaven and pour out for you such blessing that there will not be room enough to receive it."

(Malachi 3:10)

Upon graduating from college, I decided that I wanted to consistently give back by tithing. So, I did. With a very fixed income at the time, I decided that I would step out on faith and trust God. You know, it was funny, when I fell on hard times and reneged on my commitment to tithe, everything that could go right went wrong! I would owe more than I earned, my car would constantly need to be repaired, and I incurred unexpected expenses frequently. However, when I recommitted to God, amazingly, my dollars would stretch and I never went without.

After learning this simple lesson early on in life, I decided to remain faithful in the area of tithing and to be a blessing to others no matter what. Years later, I have never gone one day without. This is still my testimony today!

Can you really afford to tithe?

The thought of giving up money can be very fearful. At least it was for me. I questioned whether I would be able to meet my needs. I would ask myself, "Does the concept of tithing really make sense? How could God expect me to live off of only 90% of my income?" I thought to myself, "Really God? I am barely making ends meet now!"

And I know that I am not alone. When I speak to others about tithing, many are fearful that they would be unable to make it if they commit to God. However, the reality is, you can't afford not to. God tells us in His Word, He will open for you the windows of heaven and pour out for you such blessing that there will not be room enough to receive it (Malachi 3:10).

Trust Him in advance

Deciding to trust God with your finances requires a faithful commitment to God. It means even when your change is "strange" and times are rough, you will still commit to what God has already instructed you to do.

Now listen, when you decide to tithe and really trust God, there may be distractions that get you off track. But warning – this is only a test! Stay true to your commitment and you will see God's blessings in your life.

Really, there is no way around it. I can recall countless times being a blessing to others and within days receiving financial blessings unexpectedly. Now please understand, I do not tithe for what I can receive, but more importantly I do it out of my obedience to Him.

I know there will be many people who may think you are crazy and others who will never be able to understand it. This is why many people are more willing to give up their time but less willing to give up their money. Please know, once you make a commitment to God, He promises in His Word that He will be committed to you.

Daily Prayer: Heavenly Father, we come to You today worshipping You in spirit and truth (John 4:23-24). We thank You for allowing us to see another day with You. We thank You for Your goodness and ask You to humbly bless our financial prayer requests (declare your prayer requests). We know we do not have to worry about our finances because You say if we bring our tithes, You will pour out a blessing we will not have room enough to receive (Malachi 3:10). Your Word also tells us, You will rebuke the devour for our sake (Malachi 3:11). God we declare and decree right now, our finances are lining up with Your Word. We thank You for doing so and declare and decree it is done. In the name of Jesus Christ of Nazareth, we pray (John 14:14). Amen.

Reflection Questions

1. If you have not committed to tithing, what has stopped you from being obedient in this area of your life?

_____
_____
_____
_____

2. Was there a time when you did not tithe? If so, how did you commit to make a change?

_____
_____
_____
_____

3. How has tithing made a difference in your life?

_____
_____
_____
_____

4. What steps can you take today to start tithing in your life?

_____
_____
_____
_____

Take Action

What is the first thing you do at payday?

At the onset of each payday (or upon receipt of new cash flows), take a few minutes to really sit down and plan your finances for the upcoming period. First, commit to praying over your finances and seeking God's wisdom. Get an understanding of the purpose of each dollar that comes into your possession. Next, before spending on anything, commit to paying your tithes. Stand on His Word knowing that He will bless you in the area of finances.

Challenge #1

Have you partnered with God concerning your finances? On this day, I challenge you to seek God first regarding your finances. Pray the financial healing prayer (located in Commandment #10 as the daily prayer). Next, commit to God by paying your tithes. In Malachi 3:10, God says, "Test Me!" Try Him today! He promises if you trust in Him, He will do the unthinkable in your financial life.

Notes:

Commandment # 2 - Plan for your financial future

Scripture Reading: "The plans of the diligent lead surely to plenty, but those of everyone who is hasty, surely to poverty."

(Proverbs 21:5)

How is your financial future? In Proverbs 21:5, God tells us the plans of the diligent will lead to profit, however, those who are hasty or fail to plan will certainly lead to poverty. In order to obtain your financial healing, you must implement a plan for your finances. This way, attacks of unexpected expenses, unemployment, natural disasters, illnesses and other adverse financial events will not cause your financial house to be shaken.

The power of writing

It is essential to write your financial goals on paper. You must understand that there is something powerful about putting your thoughts on paper. During my college years, I decided to write my career goals to become a certified public accountant (CPA), an Internal Revenue Service (IRS) criminal investigator and to obtain my master's degree. Don't ask me why I wanted to become an investigator but hey, the glamour of the job appealed to me!

However, not only did God bless me with each of these goals, but He has also continued to do so much more. Since then, there are many financial, career, relationship and other goals I have received from God, by simply writing my petitions on paper. This is also proven in God's Word. Habakkuk 2:2 instructs us to write the vision and make it plain so that he may run who reads it.

Declare and decree

Wake up each morning declaring your financial goals will come to pass. Post your goals somewhere you can view them throughout the day. Whether you post them on your refrigerator or vanity mirror, allow your goals to serve as a constant reminder where you are going. Seeing these visually can also encourage you when deciding whether to purchase a pair of shoes, tickets to your favorite sports game or your morning coffee latte. Understand how making these small sacrifices may ensure your children's education is funded, reduce your financial burdens or allow you the ability to live a financial healing lifestyle.

Begin to speak God's Word into the atmosphere, knowing death and life are in the power of the tongue (Proverbs 18:21). Declare that God is supplying all of your needs (Philippians 4:19), you are the lender and not the borrower (Deuteronomy 28:12) and more importantly, all things are possible if you simply believe it (Mark 9:23)!

Daily Prayer: Heavenly Father, we come to You today worshipping You in spirit and truth (John 4:23-

24). Your Word tells us to write our visions and make it plain, so that it may come to pass (Habakkuk 2:2). We declare our visions are certain to come to pass. We expect that our debts are cancelled and dissolved, we have more than enough and we are operating according to a plan for our finances. We ask the Holy Spirit to guide us so that we can move in the direction You require of us as it relates to our finances. We pray for wisdom and surrender our plans to You knowing that although we may make a plan, You have the best plan for us (Proverbs 16:9). We ask that You continue to lead and guide us. In the name of Jesus Christ of Nazareth, we pray (John 14:14). Amen.

Reflection Questions

1. Have you identified your financial goals? Do you know where you want to be this time next year, in the next five years or years to come?

_____
_____
_____
_____

2. What steps must you take in order to make your goals a reality? What ways can you achieve them?

_____
_____
_____
_____

3. How can you hold yourself accountable? Consider requesting your partner to hold you accountable.

_____
_____
_____
_____

4. What can you do to remind yourself of your goals each day to help you stay the course?

_____
_____
_____
_____

Take Action

Do you have a P.O.W.E.R. goal?

Of course it is a great idea to say I will have a sum of money saved by this time next year. However, if you are not taking action you will be unable to reach your financial goals. The Bible also tells us that faith without works is dead (James 2:17). This means you have to not only pray, but put in work!

In my classes, I encourage participants to put P.O.W.E.R. behind their actions. P.O.W.E.R. stands for

- **P**ray about your plan
- **O**ne specific goal
- **W**rite it down
- **E**mpower it with action
- **R**eview and read it daily

Challenge #2

So what is your P.O.W.E.R. goal? On this day, I challenge you to make it a reality! Pray about your financial plan. And while you may have a few goals in mind, I want you to focus on one specific goal and write it down. Next, list ways to empower your goals with action. Finally, place your P.O.W.E.R. goal somewhere you can review and read it daily. Work in faith daily to bring your goal to pass!

Notes:

Commandment # 3 - Let your budget inspire you

Scripture Reading: *"For which of you, intending to build a tower, does not sit down first and count the cost, whether he has enough to finish it— lest, after he has laid the foundation, and is not able to finish, all who see it begin to mock him, saying, 'This man began to build and was not able to finish?'"*

(Luke 14:28-30)

We hear it all the time... we must spend within our budgets, but what does that really mean? **Many people spend aimlessly without preparing a budget and as a result, they usually come up short in their financial goals.** Trust me, I know. There have been many times in my life when I figured I would just "wing it" or spend according to my feelings. However, this type of attitude got me nowhere. It wasn't until God began to deal with me that I decided I would commit to a budget. Then and only then, did I see changes in my finances.

Creating a budget

A **budget** is simply a listing of expected income and expenses for a period of time. A budget should be prepared at each payday or monthly with the understanding that it is a flexible and moving document. You should budget for all expected expenses, which includes recurring expenses, such as utility bills, groceries, mortgage, insurance and other expenses that you will incur for the month.

Don't forget to also budget for items that you may pay infrequently, such as your annual property taxes or a quarterly insurance bill. Setting aside a few bucks toward these annual expenses can prevent "panic mode" when the bill is due. For example, if your property taxes are due annually, consider budgeting for a monthly amount to make certain you are able to cover these expenses when they are due.

A budget serves as a roadmap to help reach financial goals. No matter if your desire is to pay for your kids to go to college or simply become debt free at a certain age, your chances to achieve your financial desires are better if you simply prepare and live within your budget.

Get inspired

Now this may seem out of the norm to some, but I am a visionary type of person. Not only do I prepare a monthly budget, but I also enjoy preparing an inspirational budget. **You will be amazed by the power of simply writing your thoughts on paper and how your vision is certain to come to pass.** It is inspired from one of my favorite scriptures from the Bible, "Then the Lord answered me and said: 'Write the vision and make it plain on tablets, that he may run who reads it.' " (Habakkuk 2:2).

It is my little inspiration to envision what I desire my future budget will be. I call it my inspiration for several different reasons. It provides me a clear vision to determine where I am headed; inspiration to keep pressing knowing I will obtain the victory; and a constant reminder to understand small sacrifices will provide big rewards in the future. **Consider putting your inspirational budget somewhere you can see it each and everyday.**

More importantly, if you want to obtain victory over your financial life, consider making steps toward living within your budget, creating an inspiration budget and you will see God do a great thing in your life!

Daily Prayer: Heavenly Father, we come to You today worshipping You in spirit and truth (John 4:23-24). Father God, we thank You for every dollar You have placed in our possession. We declare this day going forward, we will not spend a dime without first consulting You. We ask that You give us wisdom to not only create a budget but also give us the discipline to remain within our financial boundaries. We will commit a portion of our earnings to furthering the kingdom through the giving of our tithes and offerings. In the name of Jesus Christ of Nazareth, we pray (John 14:14). Amen.

Reflection Questions

1. How often do you budget? What steps can you take to ensure you budget consistently?

_____
_____
_____
_____

2. What ways do you ensure that you monitor your spending?

_____
_____
_____
_____

3. Have you taken time to review your budget to determine whether you have a surplus or deficit? What expenses can be eliminated or reduced?

_____
_____
_____
_____

4. What do you want your inspirational budget to look like in the future? What will that require?

_____
_____
_____
_____

Take Action

You make a lot, but how much do you keep?

Do you earn much, but save very little? While you may make a great income, the true blessing is how much you can keep! Keeping more of your hard earned cash is only achieved through budgeting and monitoring your spending. A great tool to use is what I like to refer to as the ABCs to budgeting.

After you commit to paying your tithes, separate your pay as follows:

(A) Automate your pay. Each payday or monthly, have a set amount of cash drafted into a savings account.

(B) Budget for your bills. Next, pay your bills at the each payday, which I refer to as paycheck budgeting.

(C) Cash for everything else. Lastly, after you have tithed and paid your bills, the money that remains is your cash for everything else.

Challenge #3

So what amount will you allocate to your ABCs? On this day, I challenge you to create a budget based on these principles. Identify the amount you will set aside for savings, bills and cash for discretionary spending.

Notes:

Commandment # 4 - Be prepared for what tomorrow brings

Scripture Reading: "And at midnight a cry was heard: 'Behold, the bridegroom is coming; go out to meet him!' Then all those virgins arose and trimmed their lamps. And the foolish said to the wise, 'Give us some of your oil, for our lamps are going out.' But the wise answered, saying, 'No, lest there should not be enough for us and you; but go rather to those who sell, and buy for yourselves.' And while they went to buy, the bridegroom came, and those who were ready went in with him to the wedding; and the door was shut."

(Matthew 25:6-10)

On August 29, 2005, who knew an evacuation order would be the last time I would see New Orleans, as I knew it. A "hurricane trip" as I referred to it happened frequently, so why would this time be anything different? My "hurricane trips" would usually turn out to be short vacations and time off from work, but this time I would never be able to return back to life, as I knew it. Hurricane Katrina destroyed my home, my personal belongings and left me homeless. More importantly, I was now faced with many financial uncertainties.

Fortunately, after graduating from college and starting my first job, I started saving for the unexpected. Not realizing the unexpected would arrive so soon, but it did. The Bible warns us to plan (Proverbs 21:5). This applies to all areas of our lives. Therefore, no matter what, commit to preparing yourself financially for the unexpected.

Use wisdom

What we have to understand is that in this life some rain must fall, therefore we have to use wisdom as it relates to our finances. Wisdom is one of the key foundations to successfully obtaining a financial healing. In James 1:5, it tells us we can ask God for wisdom and He will generously provide it to us. **We must be wise with every dollar that we encounter. This requires us to be good stewards over our finances and set aside a portion of each dollar that comes into our possession.** The Bible tells us even the ants, although they are not strong, prepare and store for the future (Proverbs 30:25). Are we not worth more than ants?

Pay yourself first

After paying your tithes, you have to pay yourself first. This requires treating yourself as if you were a bill. Whether it is a few dollars or hundreds, no one deserves your money more than you! Whether it is $20 or $200, it is important you are consistent, and before long you will be amazed how quickly the money will add up.

Our scripture reading for today warns us about the consequences of being unprepared (Matthew 25:6-10). We witness ten women who set out on the journey, but only half were able to conquer it. What about you? Would an unexpected expense set you back or would you be able to continue on your financial journey?

So as you set out on your financial journey, remember be prepared financially for the unexpected. It is not a matter of what if, but when rain will fall. Simply put, we have to be prepared for whatever tomorrow brings.

Daily Prayer: Heavenly Father, we come to You today worshipping You in spirit and truth (John 4:23-24). Your Word warns us to plan for the unexpected (Proverbs 21:5). We declare and decree we will set aside a portion of each dollar for a rainy day. We ask that You give us wisdom that we would be better stewards over our money and resources. We thank You that we have more than enough and are grateful for all that You have blessed us with. We pray that You continue to order our steps and direct our paths as it relates to our finances. We thank You in the name of Jesus Christ of Nazareth, we pray (John 14:14). Amen.

Reflection Questions

1. Am I committed to saving enough for a rainy day? If not, what steps can I take?

_____
_____
_____
_____

2. What steps have I taken to commit to prepare financially for the unexpected (savings, insurance, financial plans, etc.)?

_____
_____
_____
_____

3. Do I periodically review my insurance policies and accounts to ensure they are updated?

_____
_____
_____
_____

4. Do I periodically review accounts to update beneficiaries?

_____
_____
_____
_____

Take Action

Are you prepared for an unexpected expense?

In Proverbs 30:25, the reading tells us the ants are a people not strong, yet they prepare for the summer. Are you seriously preparing for your financial future? Aren't we much more stronger and smarter than an ant? If the ant could prepare for the future, certainly with God's help, we can too.

Preparation is defined as the act of doing something to get ready for an act or undertaking. Where do you see yourself going in life? It is not enough to say you will retire at a certain age without taking the necessary steps in order to do so. So, where should you begin?

First, you have to begin with an understanding that the only way to your financial healing is being able to weather the financial storms that may come your way. This can only be achieved by making certain you are prepared for unexpected financial events that may happen along the way.

Challenge #4

Have you had trouble saving money in the past? Ask God for His wisdom and begin to think of different ways to save. On this day, I challenge you to look at every expense and identify one way or another to reduce or eliminate it. Consider using the money saved to beef up your emergency fund.

Notes:

Commandment # 5 - Be the lender and not the borrower

Scripture Reading: "The Lord will open to you His good treasure, the heavens, to give the rain to your land in its season, and to bless all the work of your hand. You shall lend to many nations, but you shall not borrow."

(Deuteronomy 28:12)

Often we believe God for certain areas in our lives, but fail to believe God for the possibility to live debt free. But I challenge you to change your mindset, start thinking new and believe you will obtain God's goodness as it relates to your debt.

Previously, I questioned whether I would be able to live a debt free lifestyle. I always had credit cards and wholeheartedly believed since I made my monthly payments, I was okay. However, God began to challenge me to be credit card debt free. He instructed me to purchase everything with His resources and not of the world's. This was new to me, I had always depended on my credit cards. I felt in case I ever had an emergency, I would have my many credit cards to fall back on. But God was challenging me to do something brand new – He said trust in Him with all my heart and lean not to my understanding (Proverbs 3:5-6). So I did. Reluctantly at first, I began to wean myself off my credit cards and more importantly I decided to pay each and every card off. But now I realize this is truly a blessing.

My come to Jesus moment

I first had my "come to Jesus moment" and wrote every credit card debt and small loan balance on the Debt Reduction Template[1] I created. From there, I divided each balance by twelve (12) to determine the amount I would need to pay monthly in order to eliminate my balances.

Next, I had to get creative. I thought of clever ways where I would be able to earn money. This included money earned from self-employment, hobbies, and other sources of income. For each month, I created expected additional streams of income that I fully committed to reduce my debt.

Throughout my debt reduction plan, I abided by my "just say no plan!" This simply meant, I just said no to incurring additional debt and to spending on items I really didn't need. And finally, I said yes to living within my budget.

Keep going

In addition, I kept my plan with me during the entire process. This served as a reminder to help me stay on course. Therefore when I was tempted to purchase a

---

[1] http://kemberley.com/wp-content/uploads/2013/09/Debt-Reduction-Template.pdf

new handbag or a new pair of shoes, I recalled that a few months ahead I would have a zero credit card balance.

I also need to tell you that the process was challenging and at times, I was unable to pay the amount I committed to on paper. However, these minor setbacks cannot compare to the feeling of being credit card debt free now. Also, the great thing is I am now applying this method to all areas of my life, just saying no to all debt and now believe it is possible to be totally debt free!

Daily Prayer: Heavenly Father, we come to You today worshipping You in spirit and truth (John 4:23-24). Father God, we declare our debts and loans are cancelled and dissolved. We believe that nothing is impossible with You and You can do the unthinkable in our lives. We declare we are the lenders and not the borrowers (Deuteronomy 28:12). We will utilize our gifts, talents and resources creatively to reduce our debt burdens, just like the widower who utilized the oil in her possession to pay off her debtors (2 Kings 4). We thank You as we move forward on this journey that we will use wisdom and not fall into unnecessary debt again. We thank You for the many blessings that You have bestowed upon us and thank You for all that You have blessed us with. In the name of Jesus Christ of Nazareth, we pray (John 14:14). Amen.

Reflection Questions

1. What do you have in your possession that you can utilize to pay off debt?

_____
_____
_____
_____

2. When will you have your "come to Jesus" moment? What steps can you take to create additional streams of income?

_____
_____
_____
_____

3. How can you start anew concerning your debts? Are there creditors you can speak with to reduce payments or make payment arrangements?

_____
_____
_____
_____

4. When was the last time you reviewed your credit report? Or disputed any errors or inaccuracies?

_____
_____
_____
_____

Take Action

What's in your possession?

In 2 Kings 4:1-7, there was a certain widower whose husband left her family in debt. Because she was unable to pay, the creditors sought to take her sons as bondsmen. Therefore, she sought wisdom from Elisha to determine what to do. He asked her what did she have in her possession.

This statement is profound because many times we have everything we need to get out of debt, however we sometimes overlook it. This widower realized that she did have oil that she could sell to generate income. But what about you? What do you have in your possession? Can a part-time job help you get out of debt? Can your God given talents generate additional income? Or can selling slightly used items help earn extra cash? Whatever it is, know that each of us have something. We simply need to ask God for His wisdom to understand what it is.

Challenge #5

On this day, I challenge you to take time to determine what is in your possession. Consider hobbies, self-employment, part-time jobs and other options. Also, consider reviewing past tax returns for missed deductions to find additional cash. Make a listing of items that can generate additional income and create a plan of action to achieve it.

Notes:

Commandment # 6 - Don't hide your money in a napkin

Scripture Reading: "Then another came, saying, 'Master, here is your mina, which I have kept put away in a handkerchief. 21 For I feared you, because you are an austere man. You collect what you did not deposit, and reap what you did not sow.' 22 And he said to him, 'Out of your own mouth I will judge you, you wicked servant. You knew that I was an austere man, collecting what I did not deposit and reaping what I did not sow."

(Luke 19:20-22)

In this passage, we find a noblemen who leaves money to each of his ten servants upon his departure. He instructs each of them to invest the money until he returns. Upon his return, he calls each of the ten servants to determine how much money each has gained by investing.

He finds that the first and second servant invested wisely. As a result, they both obtained a gain on their investment. Because of this, he blessed those servants and made them ruler over a number of cities. However, when the noblemen questioned the third servant, he finds that servant did not invest the money, but simply kept the money tucked away in a napkin. This is no different in our lives. As a steward of God's resources, He too will ask what we did with our time, possessions and resources.

Be faithful over little

Just as in this passage, **God requires us to be good stewards over all that He has placed in our care.** It is our responsibility to ensure our gifts, talents and more importantly, our money grows. So, my question for you is, how much money are you hiding in a napkin?

I can recall having the opportunity to speak with a friend who informed me about her fear of investing. Because of the ups and downs in the market, she decided to simply not invest at all. As a result, she is more comfortable with conservative financial products such as certificate of deposits (CDs) and money market accounts, which pay little to no interest.

But the reality is, just as the servant we read about in the passage, if we are not growing our resources, we are not exercising good stewardship over what God has given us. Keep in mind, if you have financial goals, you can't afford not to invest. Of course investing can be risky, but placing your money in "safe" financial products, such as CDs, have risks as well. These products are subject to inflation risk, which is the risk your money will be unable to keep up with today's dollar. As a result, you really are losing money due to the loss of purchasing power.

Understanding whether you should invest is a matter of what your financial goals are and your time horizon. Of course, if you need the money for emergencies or for a down payment on a home in the next year or so, it may not be a good idea to invest these funds in risky assets. Since the market is risky, especially in the short term, a quick drop in the market could diminish your investment. However, if time is on your side, investing for the long term is a great idea, because losses could possibly be offset by future gains.

Where to start?

If you are afraid of investing or simply have a fear of investing, I challenge you to become educated. There are a ton of resources for beginning investors to help obtain knowledge concerning the stock market. Also, it is also just as important to get your personal finances in order before investing. This means building your emergency fund first and of course paying off high interest debt.

Building your emergency fund is essential because it is not wise to invest funds that should be allocated to savings. Lastly, paying down high interest debt is also a great money move. Reducing this debt burden can not only decrease the amount you owe but also can help you save more money by eliminating finance charges.

Daily Prayer: Heavenly Father, we come to You today worshipping You in spirit and truth (John 4:23-24). Father God, we declare that we will exercise stewardship over every dollar You put into our possession. We ask that You give us the necessary wisdom, education and knowledge to invest according to Your will. In Your Word, You tell us to study to show ourselves approved (2 Timothy 2:15). We ask that we do not move before seeking You first in our finances, so that we know that it is God approved. In the end, we will choose the right direction and path for our resources. We continue to thank You for Your continual blessings, for our finances, talents and resources. We ask that You continue to lead us in this area of our lives. In the name of Jesus Christ of Nazareth, we pray (John 14:14). Amen.

Reflection Questions

1. Have you established an emergency fund?

_____
_____
_____
_____

2. Do you have high interest debts you need to pay prior to investing?

_____
_____
_____
_____

3. If you have a retirement account, have you taken time to understand how the funds are invested? Or evaluate the fees?

_____
_____
_____
_____

4. What steps can you take to learn more about investing?

_____
_____
_____
_____

Take Action

Every dollar has a purpose!

Throughout life, we will have the opportunity to obtain many financial blessings. But it will be up to us to understand what and what not to do with the money we receive. When we understand that every dollar has a purpose, it is then we obtain financial healing upon our lives.

Understanding this, you have to set your financial house in order. First, establish an emergency fund for unexpected expenses. Next, take a good look at your debt and put a plan in place to better manage it. Consider eliminating high interest debt to save money. In Proverbs 24:27, it tells us that we should first plan and prepare and then begin to build our house. The same holds true with our finances, set your financial foundation but don't stop there. Begin to build your wealth by investing properly. This is where true financial healing begins.

Challenge #6

Have you set your financial house in order? Before investing, it is a good idea to do so. On this day, I challenge you to not only set your financial house in order but commit to learning more about investing. There are many tools and resources that can guide you in selecting the right investments that align with your time horizon, risk and financial goals.

Notes:

Commandment # 7 - Let your finances be decent and in order

Scripture Reading: "Let all things be done decently and in order."

(1 Corinthians 14:40)

The true way to conquer finances is first to get a handle on it all. How can you be victorious in this area if you simply do not know whom you owe, the amount you can expect or what you are required to pay? Our scripture reading reminds us that everything we do must be done not only decently but also in order.

Throughout the Bible, you will see Jesus performed all things decently and in order. Nothing shows us this better than the passage Mark 6:30-44. In this passage, we see that even before Jesus turned five loaves of bread and two fish into a sufficient amount to feed thousands, He first ordered the people to sit into groups of fifties and hundreds. He then gave thanks to God and was able to feed five thousand people and also had twelve baskets of food remaining.

Each month we are bombarded with bills in our inbox, smartphone, or mail. And of course with anything, without having a sound system in place, we can easily be overwhelmed. If your bills have gotten the best of you, here are few a steps to help manage your monthly bills.

Create a system

Having a system for your bills is key. A great idea is to pay your bills according to your pay schedule – paycheck budgeting. For example, if you are paid on the 1st and 15th, you may want to pay your bills on the same dates. Let's say for instance if a bill is due on the 7th, paying this bill on the 1st will not only reduce late fees, but also give you peace of mind knowing this bill has already been paid.

Establish a financial home

For each financial document that comes into your possession, create a place for it. This may require setting up a file or electronic folder for tax expenses, bank statements, insurance, monthly bills and other financial documents that you may encounter. This way, if you are in need of a document for tax or insurance purposes or simply need to verify income for a loan request, these items can be easily accessible to help you in your financial journey.

Prepare a bill calendar or go auto

It doesn't matter where or how, but writing your bills and due dates somewhere visible can help you better manage your bills. Consider using a bill calendar or checklist to really get a handle on your bills. Your bill calendar should include a checklist you can mark once the bills are paid. Additionally, consider whether setting up auto payments for recurring bills will work for you. But be mindful – if the amount of your bill varies from month to month, you may want to consider paying it manually.

Reduce them

Of course bills could be overwhelming, but there is something you can do about it. After you have taken the time to write your bills, review each one to determine whether you can eliminate or reduce it. This will not only help you better manage your bills but in the long run, help save you money as well!

Daily Prayer: Heavenly Father, we come to You today worshipping You in spirit and truth (John 4:23-24). Father God, we ask that You give us wisdom and knowledge so that we can operate decently and in order as it relates to our finances (1 Corinthians 14:40). We declare we are no longer living in confusion financially but we have a handle over every aspect of our financial affairs. Father God put a willing and obedient spirit in us as it relates to our finances (Isaiah 1:19). We declare we are no longer in financial bondage but operate in financial freedom. We thank You for Your financial blessings over our lives. In Jesus Christ of Nazareth, we pray (John 14:14). Amen.

Reflection Questions

1. Have you created a system for your finances?

_____
_____
_____
_____

2. Are your financial documents organized? What can you do to become better organized?

_____
_____
_____
_____

3. Do you have a bill calendar or other document to serve as a reminder for upcoming bills?

_____
_____
_____
_____

4. In the event of an illness or an unfortunate mishap, do you have a listing of financial responsibilities to serve as instructions for a loved one? If not, what steps can you take to do so?

_____
_____
_____
_____

Take Action

Have the financial talk!

Shortly after my father had a stroke, I can recall sitting next to his hospital bed asking him questions such as, "Dad, who holds your mortgage? What expenses should be paid this month?"

Wow. That was a difficult time for my family and I. Not just because he had a stroke, but because it happened a few months after Hurricane Katrina. At that time, my entire family was displaced from their homes. Even more so, now I had yet another challenge. I knew I had to make certain his bills were taking care of but I didn't know where to start.

Because of this, it is important to create a **financial account checklist.** Not only should you complete this checklist, but you should have discussions with loved ones concerning your finances. This way, in the event you suffer an illness or experience a natural disaster, you and your loved ones will have one less thing to worry about.

Challenge #7

Have you had discussions with a trusted loved one concerning your finances? On this day, I challenge you to ask God to reveal to you whom this person should be. Take time to discuss important matters that would need to be taken care of in the event of sickness, death or any other unfortunate event.

Notes:

Commandment # 8 - Be faithful over little

Scripture Reading: "He who is faithful in what is least is faithful also in much; and he who is unjust in what is least is unjust also in much."

(Luke 16:10)

Throughout life, God will bless you with a finite amount of resources. You will be blessed with only so much money, time, assets and talents. With each blessing God has given you, He expects you to be a good steward of what He has blessed you with.

Faithfulness creates fruitfulness

How can you ask God to bless you with millions if you can't take care of a thousand? Real financial healing takes place when you learn how to take care of the little that God has blessed you with already. Think about it, how can you desire a large home, but fail to take care of your small apartment? If you want to really see blessings in your life, you have to learn to take care of small matters before He can trust you with larger ones!

Consider your ways

One of my favorite passages in the Bible reminds us to consider our ways! Haggai 1:6-7 reminds us that while we may earn much, in some cases we have very little to show for it. We have to understand that although it is a true blessing to earn a lot of money, the reality is if you spend just as much as you earn, the occurrence of one negative financial event can cause a financial disaster.

Learn to live on less

Take time to commit to live on less than what you earn. No matter if you are earning $20,000 or $2 million, if you are not careful about your spending habits, then you may find yourself having more month than money. After creating and reviewing your budget, look for ways to live on less of your earned income. A good rule of thumb is to first commit at least ten percent (10%) each for tithing and retirement savings, and use the remainder (80%) for housing expenses, debt, discretionary expenses, and savings.

Consider your savings off limits

From day to day, you will be faced with making decisions such as whether you should save or spend. It will seem as though no matter where you turn, there will always be an opportunity to spend your money, and less of an opportunity to save. Because of this, you have to stay committed to your budget and more importantly, consider your savings off limits. Of course, there may be times when you have to dip into your savings, but consider your savings off limits unless there is a dire need.

Always keep in mind that you never know where this life may take you. Consistently saving first before spending will help you weather adverse financial events that may come your way.

Daily Prayer: Heavenly Father, we come to You today worshipping You in spirit and truth (John 4:23-24). Father God, we ask that You give us the ability to be good stewards over our resources. You say in Your Word, if we are faithful over least we will be faithful over much (Luke 16:10). For this reason, we ask that we are mindful of all that You have placed in our possession and that we will be careful to exercise good stewardship over our resources. Please Father God, help us to consider our ways and give us the knowledge to do Your will. We declare we are no longer unfaithful over least. We thank You for doing a new thing in our lives. In Jesus Christ of Nazareth, we pray (John 14:14). Amen.

Reflection Questions

1. How can you commit to become a better financial steward?

_____
_____
_____
_____

2. What areas do you feel most convicted when spending? What can you choose to do differently?

_____
_____
_____
_____

3. Are you mindful of every dollar that you spend? What steps can you take to consider each purchase?

_____
_____
_____
_____

4. Are there areas that you can sacrifice to be a blessing to God's kingdom?

_____
_____
_____
_____

Take Action

Consider your ways

Because of our desires to spend, at one time or another, we may have found ourselves spending out of control. Nothing teaches us this better than Haggai 1:6-7, which instructs us to consider our ways! It reminds us that while we may earn much, if we are not careful, it may disappear as if we are filling our pockets with holes! Wow!

Have you ever questioned where your money went for a certain period? I mean, you started the week with a large sum, but by the end of week, you realized that you had nothing left. If we are not careful, our money will slip right out of our hands. As such, we have to be mindful of every dollar that we spend. God wants us to not only consider our ways, but not be wasteful of the resources that He has blessed us with. It is in this place, we can be a blessing to God's kingdom.

Challenge #8

Are you mindful of every dollar that you spend? On this day, I challenge you to ask God to help you to be considerate of each purchase. Select a time period to record and really evaluate every dollar that you spend. During this time, question whether a purchase is necessary or if it can be utilize for saving, investing or eliminating debt.

Notes:

Commandment # 9 – Don't cheat on your taxes

Scripture Reading: "They said to Him, 'Caesar's.' And He said to them, 'Render therefore to Caesar the things that are Caesar's, and to God the things that are God's.'"

(Matthew 22:21)

In Matthew 22:21, Jesus warns to pay unto Caesar what is due unto him. Yes, it may be easy to bump up your deductions a couple of dollars here or there, but the reality is – it really does not pay to cheat on your taxes.

Pay now or later...

While receiving a large tax refund or credit is great, having to repay this amount later is simply no fun. Often times, when we are required to repay tax refunds, the amount has already been spent. As a result, we are required to repay not only the amount due, but this may leave us vulnerable to various penalties and interest for failure to report tax information correctly.

Also, keep in mind, if the return is deemed fraudulent, hefty penalties may apply and the taxpayer could face a criminal investigation.

Ease your tax burden now

Consider reviewing your tax situation three to four times a year. During these times, determine whether it is necessary to make additional tax payments or take advantage of certain deductions to reduce or eliminate your tax liability. If you are a self-employed individual, you may be required to make estimated payments depending on the amount of income you earned.

Also, take time to review your tax withholdings to determine whether you are withholding a sufficient amount of taxes from your paycheck. If you are unsure regarding how much you should withhold from your pay, consider using a withholding calculator available on the Internet to estimate the correct number of withholdings. Taking time to review your withholdings can ensure you are not bombarded with an unwanted tax bill at tax time.

Explore payment options

If you owe taxes, do not be afraid. Contact the taxing authority to explore payment options. If you do not have the ability to pay your taxes in full, consider setting up an installment agreement. An installment agreement allows you to make payments over a period of time, but keep in mind there is usually a start-up fee and interest may still accrue over your payment period.

Daily Prayer: Heavenly Father, we come to You today worshipping You in spirit and truth (John 4:23-

24). Father God, we ask that You help us with our finances. Provide us with wisdom so we can reduce our tax burdens. Give us the ability to pay what is required from us to satisfy our tax liabilities. Help us to operate efficiently and effectively as it relates to our finances. We declare and decree we are prepared to meet any tax obligations we may face. We know that You are providing us with a plan to see ourselves through. We thank You for all that You have done. In Jesus Christ of Nazareth, we pray (John 14:14). Amen.

Reflection Questions

1. Do you have an understanding of the correct amount of withholdings that should be taken from your pay?

___

2. Do you consider taxes as an expense when budgeting for both business and personal finances?

___

3. Throughout the year, do you take advantage of tax deductions that can reduce your tax burden? What can you do to ensure you are doing so?

___

4. Do you keep records and receipts that can help you at tax time? What can you do to ensure you have proper documentation each year?

___

Take Action

Don't go chasing waterfalls

My mom often tells us, "All money is not good money." While it didn't really resonate with me as a young person, I now know what she means.

Obtaining a financial healing is much more than obtaining a financial gain "by any means necessary." In fact, it actually requires the opposite. In Proverbs 13:11, it reminds us that wealth obtained by fraud or hastily shall dwindle away. Therefore, we have to question whether a financial gain aligns with God's Word. If you have to do anything that is not of God, chances are this money will simply decrease in the future. It is only honest gains that will stand the test of time. Simply put, don't go chasing waterfalls!

Challenge #9

Are there financial gains that are outside of God's will? Whether it is being dishonest to receive an additional cash flow or not reporting taxable income to save a buck or two, you have to make a change. On this day, I challenge you to align your financial affairs with the Word of God. It is in this place where you will obtain your true financial healing.

Notes:

Commandment # 10 - Make wiser financial decisions

Scripture Reading: "If any of you lacks wisdom, let him ask of God, who gives to all liberally and without reproach, and it will be given to him."

(James 1:5)

Just like you would seek wisdom before deciding whom to marry, taking a new job, or agreeing to a business deal, you should also seek Him in regards to your finances. It is not enough to go "half at it" at your finances month after month. God reminds us in His Word, that He can provide us with wisdom, if we simply ask (James 1:5).

Seek wisdom

Not only should you ask for wisdom, but make it a priority to obtain wisdom for your finances. This could be achieved through personal research, hiring a financial professional or simply seeking someone who exhibits great stewardship over his or her finances.

In life, you will be required to make many decisions regarding personal finances. Whether it is to purchase a home, establish short and long term goals, save for retirement or other issues, in life you will have to navigate through your many financial decisions. The great thing to know is God has already provided the necessary tools to tackle these decisions.

Are you wearing the badge of God?

There are five principles required to handle life's financial decisions. I like to refer to them as the B-A-D-G-E! A badge is defined as a means of identification. It lets people know whom you identify with. When you are heading through life and have to make a difficult decision, you have to make certain you are wearing the B-A-D-G-E of God!

So, let us look at what the B-A-D-G-E stands for!

B – Budget

In order to get the most out of your finances, you have to create and stick to a budget. Not just every now and then, but you must budget consistently. **Budgeting provides an understanding of the purpose of every dollar that comes into your possession.** Not only does a budget give you an understanding of how to use your money, but it also provides a blueprint of what you can or cannot afford.

A- Assets

Everyone has the ability to earn money, but increasing your wealth demonstrates financial healing. Wealth is defined as your assets minus your liabilities. Thus, the more assets and the less liabilities - the better! Building wealth is the gateway to opportunities. Wealth allows for creating entrepreneurship opportunities, funding your dependents' education, purchasing a home and leaving an inheritance for your children's children!

D - Debt

Debt is the enemy of any financial healing. Having too much debt or using debt unwisely can cost more than you bargained for. Of course, there are some debts you may have to obtain in life. However, there are other forms of debt you should simply stay away from. **Using debt can either enhance your financial life or destroy it.** Be mindful of every loan, credit card, or mortgage you obtain. Determine whether the debt will move you closer to your financial healing or further away.

G – Goals

If you don't know where you are going, you won't know how to get there. Many people do not use a holistic approach when it comes to finances and as a result they have investments or assets that do not align with their goals. Know both your short term and long term goals and identify how you will get there. Simply put, create a plan for your money and even more importantly – for your life!

E – Earnings

While wealth builds opportunities, enhancing your earning potential is also key to success. Earnings provide a gateway to be able to build a better financial life. Creating multiple streams of income and increasing your potential to earn more will allow you to obtain a financial healing. Lastly, make certain to partner with God with your earnings. Commit to tithing and stand on His promises, knowing He will open the windows of heaven for you!

So what B-A-D-G-E are you wearing? Will you wear God's badge and be identified as a good steward over your finances? Or will the world not recognize your financial stewardship because of the financial mistakes you are making?

The Financial Healing Prayer

KEMBERLEY.COM
Wear the BADGE (A personal finance blog for the young, saved and savvy!)

FINANCIAL HEALING PRAYER

Heavenly Father, we come to You worshipping You in spirit and truth **(John 4:23-24)**. We ask today for forgiveness for our financial mistakes. We thank You for giving us another chance to be better financial stewards. You say in Your Word, if we are faithful over little, we will be trusted with much **(Luke 16:10)**. We declare, this day going forward, we will operate with a financial plan **(Luke 14:28-30)**. We declare that we will set aside a portion of every dime that comes into our possession, so that we may prosper **(1 Corinthians 16:2)**. We promise to be diligent in both our financial and business affairs **(Proverb 10:4)**. We thank You for all of our financial blessings and declare that we are content with what You have already blessed us with **(Hebrews 13:5)**. We declare from this day forward to be the lender and not the borrower **(Deuteronomy 15:6)** and that our debts are cancelled and dissolved. We promise to tithe and give to those in need **(Proverbs 21:26)**, knowing we will receive **(Malachi 3:10)**. We cease from worrying because we know You will supply all our needs according to Your riches **(Philippians 4:19)**. God we know in all things we will prosper even in the land of drought **(Jeremiah 17:8)**. In Jesus Christ of Nazareth's name, we pray, Amen **(John 14:14)**.

KEMBERLEY.COM © 2013

Reflection Questions

1. Budgeting - List one action step you can take to help you stick to your budget.

_____
_____
_____
_____

2. Assets - What ways can you increase your net worth?

_____
_____
_____
_____

3. Debt - Determine what steps you can take to create additional income to reduce your debt.

_____
_____
_____
_____

4. Goals/Earnings - List one short-term or long-term financial goal. What action steps can you incorporate in your lifestyle to achieve it?

_____
_____
_____
_____

Take Action

The pillars of financial healing

From the very moment I read Proverbs 30:24-28, I immediately scribbled in my Bible – the pillars of finances. This passage speaks of key financial principles - preparation, foundation, and discipline.

In this passage, we are reminded that although ants are small, they still prepare for tomorrow. Also, although conies are feeble creatures, yet they still create a solid foundation. Finally, while the locusts do not have a leader, they are wise enough to have self-discipline.

We too should apply these pillars to our financial lives. As such, we should commit to better preparing for tomorrow by budgeting, saving for a rainy day and investing. We must create a solid foundation by applying God's wisdom daily to our finances. And lastly, we have to be discipline with our funds by being content with what God has already blessed us with. Thus making a firm commitment to not spend beyond our means.

Challenge #10

What are the financial principles you stand on? On this day, I challenge you to commit daily to apply these principles to your life. Before spending on your desires, question whether you have set aside funds for emergencies, met financial responsibilities and sought His wisdom. This is where true wisdom takes place!

Notes:

Conclusion

So, are you willing to follow *The Ten Commandments to a Financial Healing*, to obtain victory? Let us recap!

The Ten Commandments to a Financial Healing

1. **Put God first in your finances**
   This requires seeking God first. Ask Him for His wisdom and guidance before you spend.

2. **Plan for your financial future**
   You must have a plan for your finances. Take time to write your vision for your finances and the steps it will take to make it come to pass.

3. **Let your budget inspire you**
   Not only create and follow a budget, but create an inspirational budget. Your inspirational budget is what you desire your future budget to look like.

4. **Be prepared for what tomorrow brings**
   In this life, some rain must fall. As such, you have to be prepared to weather the storm. No matter what, commit to save something from each paycheck.

5. **Be the lender and not the borrower**
   While there may be times in life where you have to use debt, you must be careful obtaining unnecessary debt. Be mindful of every debt you commit to.

6. **Don't hide your money in a napkin**
   The key to building wealth and reaching your financial goals is investing. Consider educating yourself or seeking a financial professional to learn more about investing.

7. **Let your finances be decent and in order**
   Bringing order to your finances is important to obtaining a financial healing. If your finances are in disarray, it will be difficult to reach your financial goals. Take time to organize your finances.

8. **Be faithful over little**
   Whether it is a dollar or thousands of dollars, God requires us to be good stewards. Real financial healing takes place when we are obedient over a little. Then and only then, we will be faithful over much!

9. **Don't cheat on your taxes**
   Take time to review your tax situation to determine what deductions or credits may be available to you. Planning ahead can help you to reduce your tax burden at tax time.

10. **Make wiser financial decisions**
    Create a system for your finances and wear the B - A -D -G -E! As such, **budget** consistently, review **assets**, reduce **debt**, set **goals** and enhance your **earnings**. More importantly, think twice before making financial decisions and seek God's face to become a better financial steward.

The Ten Financial Sins to Avoid

What has stopped you from following *The Ten Commandments to a Financial Healing?* What are financial sins that you should definitely avoid? Write them below. Discuss these with your accountability partner to hold yourself accountable.

1. _____

2. _____

3. _____

4. _____

5. _____

6. _____

7. _____

8. _____

9. _____

10. _____

My Financial Vision

Do you know where you want to go from here? What is your vision for your finances? Remember, Habakkuk 2:2 reminds us to make the vision plain and it shall run!

_____

_____

_____

_____

_____

_____

_____

_____

_____

_____

_____

Notes:

Notes:

About the author

Growing up in the heart of New Orleans, it is the different spelling of her name, family make up and unique career path, which makes Kemberley Washington – "Kem." She compares her different  experiences in life to a good bowl of gumbo. It may not looked so good going in, but simply magical coming out. The good, the bad, and the ugly, she would not change a thing.

Being raised by a single mother, who worked as a teacher, failing was not an option. Her mother taught during the day and worked various part-time jobs in the evenings to support her and her siblings. It is because of her mother's sacrifice early on, her and her siblings are successful today.

In addition to her mother, she also credits her father for whom she is today. Her father, who co-owns an architectural firm, provided her the opportunity to work as an accounting clerk during her teenage years. After graduating from Southern University and A&M College, she has had the opportunity to work with the Internal Revenue Service (IRS) as both a Criminal Investigator and a Revenue Agent. However, after realizing carrying a gun wasn't her thing, she utilized her experiences and pursued the calling on her life - to write and educate.

Today, she works as a business professor at Dillard University and has written, *21 Days of Powerful Breakthroughs, The Ten Commandments to a Financial Healing*, and is currently completing *Will you wear the BADGE? - A Financial Guide for the College Grad.* She frequently updates her *blogs, Kemberley.com and 21daysof.com. In* addition, she has contributed to *Bankrate.com, FoxBusiness.com, Yahoo Finance,* and many more. Also, she frequently appears on many major news outlets.

Made in the USA
Monee, IL
05 September 2022